LIVING IN THE TALL GRASS

Poems of Reconciliation

Chief R. Stacey Laforme

of the Mississaugas of the Credit
of the Anishinaabe

T0163899

UpRoute
Books & Media

An Imprint of
Durvile Publications

DURVILE &
UpRoute Books

UpRoute Imprint

An Imprint of Durvile Publications Ltd.
Calgary, Alberta, Canada
DURVILE.COM

National Library of Canada, Cataloging in Publications Data
Written and Illustrated by: Laforme, R. Stacey
Living in the Tall Grass: Poems of Reconciliation
1. Poetry 2. Indigenous Peoples 3. Indigenous Poetry

ISBN: 978-1-988824-05-5 (pbk) | 978-0-9689754-9-7 (ebook)
978-1-9888243-2-1 (audiobook)

The Every River Lit Series, and
The Indigenous Spirit of Nature Series

Cover back and front photography by Tara Laforme.
Typesetting and design by Lorene Shyba.

Printed in Canada. Fourth printing. 2022.

Durvile Publications would like to acknowledge the financial support of
the Government of Canada through the Canadian Heritage Canada Book Fund
and the Government of Alberta, Alberta Media Fund.

Durvile Publications recognizes the traditional territories upon which our studios rest.
The Indigenous Peoples of Southern Alberta include the
Siksika, Piikani, and Kainai of the Blackfoot Confederacy; the Dene Tsuut'ina;
the Chiniki, Bearspaw, and Wesley Stoney Nakoda First Nations;
and the Region 3 Métis Nation of Alberta.

Dedication

✍❦✍

To my wife Tara who was the inspiration for this book and to my children Gilbert, Kelly, PJ, Megan, and Ethan who support me no matter where I go or what dream I choose to chase. Also dedicated to the people who have moved in and out of my life, I have learned so much from all of you. Finally, to my brother Tony and sister Julie who live in the tall grass every day.

Contents

﹥︽﹝}﹞︽﹤

Prologue
Understanding

LIVING IN THE TALL GRASS is a statement of the challenging life that I have led and it also speaks to my connection to our Mother the Earth.

The front cover of this book talks about an Indigenous perspective and I guess that is true, as I am an Anishinaabe man. Yet I consider my poems and stories to be universal.

I write with the intent to place myself in the heart and soul of different individuals at different stages of their lives. If you can see yourself in the poems, then my intent was a success.

When I write, I become the character in the poem for the length of the poem. I may be happy, I may be sad, yet as soon as the poem is over it no longer owns me, and I no longer own it.

I will use this book to try to raise awareness of reconciliation but it is important that you begin with the basic understanding that reconciliation, in its broadest terms, speaks to understanding the world around us and understanding our place within it.

Prayer

We give thanks to the creator for
allowing this gathering
We ask that he guide us

And forgive us when we falter and disappoint
For though we aspire to greatness
we are after all only human

Grant us a clear mind, a pure heart
and courage
A clear mind to make well thought out
intelligent decisions

A pure heart to make decisions that are
without personal bias or desire
And the courage to use both a clear mind and
a pure heart in our lives

Let us set aside small differences, let us
concentrate on the real issues

Let us not be bogged down in rhetoric
let us live each day with a feeling of
accomplishment and pride

Most important let us remember we are not
enemies, nor are we adversaries
We share a similar past, a kindred spirit and
a common heritage

We must always remember the
real reason we gather
To do the right thing for our people
for our children, for our future.

Shkaakaamikwe/Mother Earth

SOONER OR LATER, the damage sustained by this planet will become irreversible, on that day you will not notice, for your life of comfort will continue, but the life of your children will change. They will face a world in chaos, a world where water is fought over, a world that cannot support the population They will face a world they did not create, a world inherited from you and me, a world they do not deserve, a place where the future is not promised.

So when you see people stand in defence of the lands and the waters, do not ask why they do what they do, instead ask why they stand alone.

The poem, "Sacred Trust" was written from the perspective of my people but I believe it should be a vision of all people and a statement that should be made when you become a new citizen of this Country.

Sacred Trust

We are the keepers of this land

She shelters and sustains us

Long after the flesh fails the spirit

We will care for these lands

Our drums will be heard upon the winds

Our voices in the rustle of the leaves

My people have a sacred trust with the land

A trust no man may break, a trust that
death cannot sever

We were here when you first stepped foot
upon this land

And here we will remain long after the last
step has disturbed her soil.

Untitled

I have seen many winters

I am not old, but neither am I young

I have stood witness as the sun rose and fell

I have seen the moon in all its glory

I have seen the children of the Earth

And the children of their children

I have protected them from the wind and rain

I have shielded them from the sun and heat

They have played and squabbled around my feet

And I have held them in my arms

They once honoured me

Sang songs to me, spoke to me

Of all the things I have come to love

It is them that I shall miss most of all

I will of course survive their passing

I will see a world without them

In time I will heal, my pain shall subside

But I shall never forget the children of the Earth

Nor shall I forget the children of their children

And how much joy they once brought
into my life

Their bodies may leave this place

But their spirit shall remain

I shall remember their songs and their drums

And I will sing for them and their place
upon our mother

I will not remember them as they are now

I will remember them in their youth, in their joy.

Peace

A river flowing slowly along, caressing the shore
A beautiful sunrise, as the birds welcome a new day

Trees whispering to each other, as the
wind moves among them
The beautiful face of grandmother moon, as she
rises majestically over the forest

The sparkle, as the young discover true love
for the first time
A smile that crosses the face of the newly wed

A good night kiss for a child, that speaks of
unconditional love
The connection between two who have spent a
lifetime in the company of each other

Peace is a calmness that radiates out from the soul
Lasting for many of us mere moments
for the lucky few a life time, and for some
seemingly unattainable

Yet, even if stolen in seconds or measured
in moments, it is a treasure
A warm caress from the creator, that promises
love and eternity

A gift we would share, a gift with no cost
and no reward
A gift from the heart, a gift of peace

A gift, from the creator
to be shared among all

Peace.

Infestation

Are we a people living in harmony with this planet
Or are we an infestation the Earth can't shake

We pollute its waters, we poison its air
we destroy its land
All this we do in the name of comfort

We torture the Earth day after day
So the car can go another mile, so we can
have a Big Mac

Day in and day out we try to kill it
Yet why do we do this, when we are so tied to it

All the Save the Planet rallies in the world
Are not going to change a damn thing

We will never quit until the planet is dead
Which amounts to mass suicide for all of us

We call Hitler the worst murderer in history
Yet we are doing global genocide

Why do we hate the Earth
When it provides us life

True it does eventually reclaim all that it gave
Dust to dust, dirt to dirt

Is this why we hate the Earth
Thanking her in ceremony for giving us life

Yet secretly hating her for eventually
taking that life away
Do we all have a subconscious desire to kill the
thing before it claims us

Or are we just a simple people unable to
comprehend what we do
A flock of sheep that accepts everything as is

Or maybe we are just an apathetic people
Who don't care about ourselves, our children

Whatever the reason, revenge, stupidity, apathy
Once the Earth is gone, so goes its infestation.

Mother Earth

I was out in the field, firing off orders of
what was to be done
When a man appeared from behind the
glare of the sun

He asked me by what right I claim this land
So I took out the paper and placed it in his hand
This gives me the right to do as I please
I own the dirt. I own the trees

This land provides me with economic prosperity
When I look upon this land it is money
as far as the eye can see

The old man looked at me with the saddest eyes
Bent and picked up a handful of dirt
and said, you actually believe those lies

In my hand I hold all that you were are
and will ever be
You may be able to lie to yourself but not to me

This gave life to you and me
And provided for everything you have and
everything you see

This is the reason for our birth
And the reason my people call this land
Mother Earth

The Earth gave you life and provided the
necessities as you grew
The Earth nurtures you and will one day reclaim you

Maybe the courts will accept that paper as true
But we both know who owns who.

The Day the Earth Cried

The Earth cried yesterday
And no one listened

They saw but they didn't care
They knew but they didn't stop

They watched, they were appalled
but they watched
They filed letters, they said excuse me
that's wrong

They told their friends, this is wrong
And the friends said yes this is wrong

And the government said it will be okay
And the people said, yeah maybe so

And the Earth cried
And the people watched

And hurricanes happened
And the weather turned treacherous

And the Earth cried
And the people watched

The oceans and seas turned against man
Everywhere in the world weather
attacked man

And the Earth cried

And the people watched

And one day the people died

And the Earth cried and nobody watched.

The thing we all share is our connection to the land. It may be buried down deep or it may rest on the surface but at one point in time, we all knew the value of the land because we all depended on her for life. We still do but we have forgotten this truth.

It is not the Indigenous peoples' responsibility to save the planet; it is our responsibility to help you reconnect to the world around you. So that together with the different gifts we have, we may save the planet.

Remember, we need the Earth she does not need us.

Gwekwaadziwin/Honesty

><一{}一<

I heard the Anishinaabe creation story at the age of fifty. It opened my eyes to why I act the way I do, why I believe the way I do.

Many beliefs I carry are from the creation story. Two things stand out in the creation story for me. The first, delineation of gender, was our Mother the Earth, which teaches us how important and valued the women should be. The second was when the creator made the Anishinaabe, he made the most beautiful creature he could imagine. That speaks to love of oneself.

It is important that we all have a sense of the history, for you cannot go forward without looking back. The following stories are difficult to hear, to feel and to live but it is where we must begin our journey.

You will read about the residential school, the sixties scoop, the impact of generational trauma. Remember this is not about guilt or blame, it is so that you can stand in our shoes for a few moments.

I dedicate this section to those who have lived through the residential school system and those who live through it still.

From Hell To Here

I cry and beg and plead to stay
Through unheard tears they drag me away

My parents stand helpless with their heads hung low
Through unspeakable pain they weep as I go

Into a room of pain and fear
Children all ripped from a life they held dear

A child of six, I awake from a horrible nightmare
With no one to comfort me, with no one to care

An adult creeps in, I listen and I pray
While another child has innocence stolen away

The nights are long and hard to take
I hear the others cry, as I lay awake

Some are taken from this evil room
Never again seen, and never gone home

I see you late at night when you think we are in bed
Dragging away bodies of the recently dead

Though the nights are evil and drawn
A fresh new terror comes with the dawn

You beat me and beat me until blood glistens
This is the only way to get savages to listen

I speak in words that my elders taught me
Whipped and abused so that I could see

My language is heathen, English is best
My life is evil, and evil must be put to rest

My beliefs are wrong yours are right
My culture stolen by the force of your might

Forced to live this way of life
Peace could come at the end of a knife

No! My people survive and learn how to cope
While there is life there is a future, there is hope

Today is here, that life is my past
But the memories and lessons you taught me will last

Your society sees me as a burden and a waste
An Indian you view as a disgrace

But the next time you judge and you
consider your stats
I am what you made me, now you live with that.

Forgiveness

He once was a man I wished to be near
Now I live each day in fear

The bruises I can try to hide
But not the pain I feel inside

I love you he says every day
I must leave, I cannot stay

I live, but I don't have a life
Is this the fate of every wife

I leave every night in my dreams
But how often I awake to my own screams

I am gone now from this place
Sadly I have lost this deadly race

Now my family weeps for me
I wish that I could make them see

Now is not the time to cry
I lived my hell before I died

My life was lived in pain and shame
Too weak to stop the one to blame

I have moved from that place of pain
And should forgive his mortal frame

Sadly I don't wish him well
I hope the man goes straight to hell.

Heartbeats

Sometimes, I wake up at night and call for you
And for a heartbeat, all is right with the world

But you're gone and you can't come home
And my world will always be chaos

I cry, because I cannot hold you, or touch you
I also cry, because for one heartbeat
you are here

I have seen you on every corner
In every window of every store

Sometimes I swear I hear your voice
But it's never you, how could it be

And though I know it can't be you
For one heartbeat, I think it is

So I find myself searching every face
Listening to every windblown word

My mind knows the truth
But allows my heart a moment of purity

And although the deception is brief
It exists, and in that second so do you

And I'm not sure if it's a blessing or a curse
How do I move on, when I see you every time I turn
my head too quick

How can I face the world knowing
you are not in it
Yet so briefly, you are

And your image gives me so much love
Yet the knowledge that it is just an image
breaks my heart

My heart breaks every night and all through the day
But I wouldn't give up the illusion to
end the pain

So for twenty-three hours and fifty-five minutes of
every day I grieve
But for five minutes, all is right in my world.

Nothing Grows in the Shadow

Perfect and innocent is the way life began
Lonely and afraid is how
I might end

I lived my childhood without a care
Until the beginning of a
private nightmare

I love the first rays of light
But how I hate the horror of night

I didn't know where to go or what to do
A mother who looked away and
a father who is you

I live with such guilt and shame
But I shouldn't own it
I wasn't to blame

Though I am grown and hold my head high
A shadow of a man still
traps me inside

I never became the soul
I should have been
Because nothing grows in the
shadow of a fiend.

Highway of Tears

I walk this path with so many others
But I walk it alone

I travel this road with those who have need
Together, side by side

We find small comfort in our shared resolve
We seek a common goal

At the end of our journey lies truth
Truth must be enough

For there will be no justice, no recompense
Nothing and everything would be too little

We have lost the greatest gift the creator can bestow
A mother, a sister, a daughter, a wife

So we continue our walk toward the truth
One painful step after another

The answer will come, the truth will come
Too little too late

We will reach our destination
But the journey never ends.

Who Is She

She is our mother, the one who dries our eyes
and loves us unconditionally

She is our grandmother who is wise
kind and gentle

She is our auntie, as close to being our mother
without being our mother as one can be

She is our sister, who shared our hurt, our pain
who we tease and who we love

She is our partner, mother of our child, she is
comfort, she is joy

She is our child, a sacred gift, with a smile to
brighten the heart, and a promise to live forever

She is a friend, to share an adventure
a tear, our deepest secret

She is every smile, she is every tear, she is the reason we are, and the reason we do what we do

She is our world, she is the world

She is our mother, our grandmother, our sister our auntie, our partner, our child, our friend

She is our light in a world shadowed by the grey of indifference

She is everything ...

Walking the Edge

I present calm and rational
To those who don't know me well

If you were to meet me, you might
think me sweet and shy
You might think to yourself, what a
really nice guy

Yet after awhile
You can tell there is something hidden
behind my smile

One minute I care about all that I see
The next I hate any who get near me

I am not talking about an angry moment
that passes away
I am talking about a pathological state where
my thoughts stay

It is a state of almost uncontrollable rage
A battle I am forced almost daily to wage

When I enter into this frame of mind
I can be as hateful or spiteful as any you could find

Sometimes the stage will end suddenly
But do not think it ends and I am free

For when the rage boils away
Hysterical laughter comes into play

A feeling of almost euphoric proportions
overcomes me
I am left feeling invulnerable and free

In this state I don't care what I do
In this state I am far more likely to
hurt me or you

I could take your life with a smile on my face
Of regret and remorse there
would be no trace

So remember, though I may have a smile
on my face
And a smile appears to have taken
anger's place

The laughter is reflex I was forced to invent
The thoughts remain with deadly intent

At the end of this cycle which can
last minutes or days
I am left exhausted and regretful, but
cannot change my ways

For a small part of me
Likes what I could be.

I Am Sorry

Dollars and programs you offer as retribution
For heinous crimes committed inside an institution

Pacify my people or ease your conscience
Yet we both know it is all pretense

Say you're sorry for what my people went through
Say you're here to help, I'll pretend to believe you

So what is your offer to make everything right
How many dollars will it take to ease your
conscience tonight

So give me your money and the good deeds
can commence
Money born in blood, and earned through the
brutalization of innocence

Yet know that if I but had the strength, I would
spit upon your money
I would turn my back on pretend words that mean
nothing to you and less to me

Let me abuse your children and grandchildren,
would a few dollars make it right

Would the money make up for even
one single night

Tonight when you go into your children's room
to check and make sure they're okay
Take a minute and think of the pain and terror
our children were forced to live everyday

Think long and hard, be honest and
tell me how you feel
Only then will I accept your apology, because I
will know your words are real

Though even true words cannot change the past
It is an honest start at long last

Until that day finally arrives
We will take your money and pretend to
believe your lies

And I will pray to the creator that my
ancestors can forgive
That we have forsaken their past and the way
they were forced to live.

My Love

There is no betrayal greater than the
abuse of one in your care
To harm one you are sworn to protect
is unfathomable

You stood before family and friends and
proclaimed undying love
You spoke with passion and conviction

You smiled when you looked over and saw
the love and admiration in your bride's eyes
The skin so perfect and smooth, those
beautiful lips

This is the woman you were meant to
spend your life with
The reason you were set upon this Earth

Yet in a moment of anger, a moment of
extreme weakness
You brutalized your wife and
cowered your child

And you were shocked by what you had done
You begged forgiveness from your wife and
god, never to do it again

And still the moments grew in time
To the point where the moments
overshadowed the rest of their lives

There is no excuse for what you have done
what you are doing
No words, no money, no gifts, nothing can
give your family back what you have taken

There is no greater evil than the
betrayal of love
There is no greater sin than to be
cast in shadow by those sworn
to hold you to the light.

Stolen Chances

The trees stand all in a row
The leaves twist, the branches move, the winds blow

The trees are tall and strong
The perfect mask for the ultimate wrong

They hide an evil deed done
A long time ago to seven little ones

Pretty little girls there were seven
All are gone I pray to heaven

Lying among the knotted roots and dirt
All moved from their place of hurt

Placed at the foot of a tree
Buried in quiet so none could see

All taken to this place
All stolen from their race

They reach towards the heavens so high
Yet among the roots is where they lie

Mute guardians of this place
Silent witness to this disgrace

The trees stand all in a row
The leaves twist, the branches move, the winds blow.

Debwewin/Truth

✻

Who do you want to be, what do you want out of life? Not what do you want to do for a living, or how much money you want to make, or how pretty will your wife or husband be, and how many children will you have, or what kind of car will you drive, but what do you want out of life, who do you want to be?

"I want to be loved and respected and live my life in a good way." Well how do I accomplish that? By being honest, speaking the truth, being kind, being respectful, and using courage and wisdom in my life.

I have been guilty many times of living my life not in accordance with the above but that is not the point, we are not perfect and will never be perfect. The point is I remember who I want to be and how I want to live my life and it is never too late to follow and find my true self!

As an individual, you should take note of who you want to be, whom you aspire to be, how you want to walk through your time on Mother Earth and base your life and values on that powerful aspiration.

Of course, your decisions will be based on the reality of what surrounds you, your everyday circumstance, but you should always consider your aspirational vision in what you do, so you know why you do what you do, to determine if you are walking in the direction of your real choice.

That vision is the real you and when we lose our way, it is because we fail to remember who we are!

As a Nation, we should follow the same methodology, who were we, who are we, and who do we want to be? Yes, of course decisions will be made on the realities of the day but without that overall vision, that overall direction, you will only think of your immediate need, wants and impacts now. That does not necessarily build a future of which we can be proud.

Some will say they have no time for this as they are too busy building a life providing for a future, but I ask for what, for when as your time is limited on this planet. Is it not more logical to live a way of life that supports the continuation of your beliefs, a world of substance, a place for the future of our children? As a Country, we must do the same. As a world, who do we want to be?

Why Am I An Indian?

Someone once asked me what
makes me an Indian
The question took me by surprise and I did not
respond, but it did make me wonder

Am I an Indian because some traveller
in history got lost?
Am I an Indian because of my appearance,
or because of where I live?

If the government says I am Indian, then
surely that is what I am
If one or both of my parents tell me
I am Indian it must be so

Does a plastic card with my name and weight on it
make me an Indian?
Am I a true Indian if I practice all the old ways and
learn my native tongue

I live on the reserve with other Indians who look
like me, surely I am one
I attend roundhouse frequently, so you
cannot say I am not

Both my parents were Indian therefore
I must be Indian
My parents have taught me to be Indian

Someone cannot make you or teach you
to be an Indian
Oh they can show you culture, clothing, language
but practice does not
an Indian make

Don't judge me by the fluid in my veins, or the
colour and shape of my skin
Don't think me Indian because I know and
practice my culture

I am an Indian because my heart screams it is so
and my soul knows it for truth
I am what I am, because my spirit will
not let me forget

So in answer to the person who wanted to know
what makes me Indian
Nothing makes me
I just am.

It Is Not Mine To Sell
Nor Is It Yours To Buy

Still I am not as adept as you, after all these years
We play your game because it is represented as
the only game
I sit across the table from you listening to your
words and I wish to express my true feelings
Yet to do so would only serve to further your cause
and reduce my people's chances
I yearn to tell you that I do not own this land, it is
not mine to sell nor is it yours to buy
The creator provided this land for my people and we
cared for it and it for us
Yet never did we profess to ownership
We are forced to say this land is ours just to acquire
something for ourselves

Is it any wonder we do not negotiate from
a stronger position
For though we say the words our hearts deny them
What would you do if I said with words what my
heart screams

Would you think my claim for compensation weak
The man who speaks in the courtrooms advises
against letting you know our feelings
You will use it against us

Yet I must speak for my honour
So I stand and tell you I do not own this land
it is a land unto itself
It is not mine to sell but I will swear it is to buy
a future for my people
I do a great injustice to the land and the creator
We do not own this land, this land owns us
I see the confusion in your face
You have no idea what I say
I sit back down and it's as if I had never spoken
The lawyer pats me on the hand and shows me
where to sign.

Dancers

They are beautiful to behold
Strong and graceful

The radiance of their regalia outshone only
By the sheer joy of the dance

Lost in the moment
Living in two worlds at once

They conjure images of days long ago
Of a way of life, that exists now, only in
moments such as these

They bring the past to life if only
momentarily
They touch the heart, tug at the soul

They are keepers of the past
A proud reminder of days gone by

They give us a glimpse of yesterday
And hope for tomorrow.

Second Chance

The sun shines, the birds sing
Who knows what today could bring

A smile almost makes it to my lips
Until I see the rope and my smile slips

I race through the open plain
The exhilaration masking the pain

I travel to the tree
To a spot none can see

This is the place where I used to play
Until darkness chased the light away

I have fond memories of this place
A smile almost breaks across my face

I throw the rope into the air.
I realize I no longer care

The rope jerks and instinctively I try
to protect my hand
Then I laugh, because I remember what
I have planned

I take one last look around
I wonder by who and when I will be found

The shadow of a tree falls across my face
I am now ready for death's icy embrace

I panic when I feel the rope pull tight
I jerk, I kick, I struggle, I fight

Betrayed by some primitive instinct to survive
I find myself still painfully alive

Will I take this as a second chance
Or get a stronger rope and different branch.

Success

How do you tell if your life was a success
What measuring unit do you use

The rich man would tell you
It's accumulated wealth

A politician would tell you
It's power that determines success

The clergy would tell you
That finding faith is the true determinate

The gregarious man would tell you
It should be measured in the number of
friends you can claim

The romantic would tell you
It's true love that makes life a success

The proud parent would tell you
It is your young that determine your success

So what is the true determinate for success
How do you measure success

If every situation is different
There cannot be one way

Each man must find his own
I measure success not by money or by friends

I ask myself if my ancestors could see me
what would they think
Would they feel pride or shame?

Through The Glass

The family all gathered around the table
I sit and I read and old Aesop's Fable

We all laugh and share
No one is afraid to admit we care

The older kids love and respect us
The little ones get a hug and go to bed
without a fuss

I whisper lovingly to my wife
You have made me the perfect life

This is what life is all about
Heaven on Earth, there is no doubt

I wish life was a Hallmark minute
But life is real and there's
no room for wishing in it

Sure the family may be gathered around the table
But I am more likely to be ripping off
an old beer label

Oh we laugh and we do share
We laugh at others because we don't care

The older boy drinks and the girl sleeps around
And the only way the younger kids go to bed
without a fuss is if they are gagged and bound

I shout at my wife get me a drink you whore
You have ruined my life and
I am not taking any more

Now this is what life is all about
Hell on Earth, there is no doubt

I wish life was a Hallmark minute
But life is real and there's
no room for wishing in it

I sit at the table all alone
The wife has died the children have grown

I don't laugh I have nothing to share
Others show friendship but more
from pity then care

Haven't seen my children since
I threw their asses out
They will amount to nothing, I have no doubt

Alcohol killed my wife
Booze destroyed my life

Now this is what life is all about
Hell must be better than this I shout.

Fool Me No More

Evil does not always come sneakily
in the back
Sometimes people swing wide the door

Eyes wide open, finished by the
hand we shook
No blame to cast, yet all to share guilt

Taken in by past and personal bias
failed by historical practice
A generation moved to grieve
a generation left to despair

A future that will be decided
by the next people
A future that is not assured, a future we set

Why, how, when did it come to this
was it inch by gradual inch
Was it foolishly trusting, ignorant neglect
or general indifference

Every step back from our beliefs
Is a push for those against those beliefs
If you don't stand for what is Right!
Then you must not cry
when you are forced to crawl

When we are tread upon by those we set above us
When the only place left to walk is on the backs
of those who lifted them up

When each step forces us down
further and further
When the stain of our failure is ground into our
clothes, our skin, our soul

Some will crumble and break, if there is still will
some will resist but all will blame another
But to find the real problem look no further than
the face that looks back at you
each morning

So concerned about what we have, what we think
we need, what we are used to, that we
chose not to see

Yet living our life does not give us the right to
jeopardize the future of those yet to be born

We may scream and rage at another, we may tell
the tales of blame to the future

Yet when our children and their children look
back upon this world they will know
where the guilt lies.

I Ran

I was not running from you
I thought I was running toward life

Once I was free I thought I would live
But guilt is an awful weight to drag around

My previous life haunted me
And never allowed the freedom I craved

So what I ran from
Was far better than what I ran to

You hate me for leaving
And I carry guilt for not staying

I have come back to try to be in your life
You recognize me but choose not to see me

And though you will never hear what I say
I must express it if only for my own sake

I didn't run because of you
I ran because of me

I was young and afraid
Afraid of getting up each morning to the
same routine

I was afraid of raising a family
The responsibility frightened
the hell out of me

I told myself I wanted something
else out of life
I told myself this is not all there is

But truthfully, mostly I was just afraid
My response, fight or flight

I lacked the conviction and courage to fight
So I took the only way left to me, flight

I know no words can change the act
No redemption can cure your pain

I just hope someday
Maybe when you reach where I was
You will not be as lacking in courage
as your father

I don't know what life would have
been like with you
But I know it was hell without you.

I Survived

I survived all your hate and your
self-righteous pride
I cried for my brothers and sisters as they died

I survived the murder of our way of life
I survived the defilement of a beautiful wife

I survived when your plagues and diseases
stole my son
Death for a boy who didn't hurt anyone

I lived through your deceit and treachery
I survived when you forced your sanctimonious
beliefs upon me

I survived the corruption of a
once-proud race
Although deception has taken pride's place

I survived when you made me an outcast
in my own land
I survived the coming of the white man!

As in all things there is a cost
Mine came in the form of a spirit lost

The man who survived, sits here and cries
A white man in a red disguise.

Truth

History is but a snapshot of the past
Taken by a camera held at a certain angle

If the camera is damaged or flawed
The picture is unfocused, unclear

If the photographer is trying to capture
a certain image
That is exactly what he captures at the
exclusion of everything else

The historian researches every picture
And bases each conclusion on fact

Yet for every story you know
There is more than one you don't

For every fact that is remembered
There is a truth left unclaimed

So how are we to know what is truth
Do we rely on a billion snapshots

No we rely on the people history has touched
You, me, our parents, our grandparents
our children

For the past can only truly be judged
By its reflection in today.

Angel

A mortal pulled an angel from heaven
Gave up forever to die everyday

Gave up the heavens to crawl in the mud
Gave up the favour of god to
incur a mortal's touch

In the name of love.

Zaagidwin/Love

OVER THE PAST FEW YEARS, I have become a hugger, much to the chagrin of my wife, who preferred it when I set a large personal boundary. I now have no issue with a hug for someone when it is offered or if I believe it is needed. I will of course always ask first.

I can no longer imagine going through life without that simple interaction with the people who move in and out of my world on a daily basis.

• • •

I was in love with the most beautiful woman. I would sit for hours watching her ready herself for bed. Then I would climb down from the tree and head home. I still believe if it was not for a court order and new blinds, true love would have won out.

It is important to remember that humour is a medicine.

My Reason

I know you have only recently come into my life
Yet it seems like I have known you forever

When I am with you
The world outside no longer exists

And when I am not with you, I think of you
And I can't think of you without smiling

I'm happier in your memory
Than I am in the midst of family and friends

Everything I enjoy in life pales in comparison
To holding your hand, touching your cheek
lying in your arms

People search endlessly
Trying to find a reason, a purpose to life

I only have to look down and see your hand
entwined with mine
To know where my reason lies.

Two Sisters, One Love

I would tell you something you may not know
You have my heart

Whether I greeted you with a smile or a frown
If you caught me laughing or in tears

If my reaction took you by surprise
If my response confused you

Never doubt my heart
Never doubt my love

Everything I did, I did for you
Every move I made, I made for you

Every child I met, was my child
Every hug I gave, was pure

To some this is a place, a reserve, to me, this is home
It is not just a place, it is my family

When the day comes
When death forces the last breath from my body

Remember that my soul is immortal
My love unending and my spirit eternal

Remember to love and care for each other
For never doubt that I will be watching

And never fear that you have lost me
For you live in my heart, as I live in yours.

This poem is in honour of a little girl
with the heart of a lion
Taetum Willow Mattice, an inspiration to all the
people she met in life.

Connection

I don't have to know you to love you
I don't have to know you to cry

I will grieve for you
I will grieve for the loss of such a gift

I will offer my prayers in your name
And I will pray for your loved ones

The thought of you
Is enough to make you part of me

My mind has created a place in my heart
A place you will now reside forever

I will miss you
I will remember

I will not be ashamed to shed my tears
A small part for you, a larger part for them,
and some for

me

I don't have to know you to love you
I don't have to know you to cry.

I Love You

She was always there to dry my eyes
She knew my heart and could sympathize

Provided comfort from a domineering dad
Dried my eyes when the pain got too bad

She always trusted and believed in me
There was something in me, only a mother could see

I must admit as sons go I wasn't the best
Many was the time I put her trust and love to test

Yet never once did she turn her back to me
Even as a rebellious youth when I fought
to break free

When I married young, when others claimed
I had ruined my life
She objected but once, then welcomed my wife

I remember her laughter, her smiling face
Of father time there was no trace

What joy she showed when I told her she was
going to be a grandmother
She loved those boys just as much as their mother

I remember the sheer terror I felt, when I had to tell
her grandsons that she had died
No words could comfort them, though I tried

I remember the day she passed away
I remember all the things I never had
the courage to say

I hope my mom knew how much I cared
Because feelings in our house were
not something we shared

We think we have all the time in the world so we
neglect to tell people how we feel
We go through life saying tomorrow, but we
never know what hand fate will deal

I know feelings and emotions are
very difficult to express
But your discomfort is small compared to your
mother's happiness

Isn't it better to take the time and
express your feelings
Then to suffer the uncertainty that
looking back brings

So damn your pride, damn what others say
Tell your mother you love her at least once a day

I know my mother knew
Yet I wish I had taken two seconds to say
I Love You.

I must explain the next couple of poems

My brother and I were iron workers the same as our dad, our uncles and our cousins. I married a woman, then my brother married her sister and moved in immediately next door to me.
What can I say, he lacked imagination.

So one day his wife, my sister in law twice, asked for a poem for their anniversary. She responded that she wanted something unique and different just for the two of them. I immediately passed over a romantic poem and said, "Here you go."
What follows is a poem I wrote for her and framed and gave to her called Love Is Blind.

The poem after that is a poem that my brother asked me to write for her birthday so that he could get even with her. It is called My Wife.

I accept no blame but they are no longer married.

Love is Blind

You used to have such long dark hair
Now your head is either silver or bare

When we met you had a muscle man shape
Now you have the shape of a grape

I used to love to rub the stubble on your chin
Now I can't tell where your head ends
and your neck begins

You were the man of my dreams
Now you're the nightmare that causes my screams

You may have changed in every way
Still if you tried to leave I'd beg you to stay

Not from love, not from fear, but because you were
so damn hard to train
I had to get the independent thinking
out of your brain

I've finally trained you to do as you're told
It's just to bad your so damn old

Just joking hon
For me, you are the only one.

My Wife

In your younger days your figure was a
sight to set hearts afire
Now you have the shape of an old spare tire

You used to have quite a rack
Now the way it hangs, I can't tell front from back

Your smile and gracious ways
used to light up the room
Now, I think you should be out riding a broom

At any dance contest, you would have won first prize
Now it would be a miracle, if you could just
lift one of your thighs

I used to love it when you would sit near
And I still do, but only after a couple of beer

You were a wild woman in bed
Now I take your pulse to make sure you're not dead

Can you believe after all this I am still here
I stay not from love, but from absolute fear

Wife I hope you know this was all in jest
To me you will always be the very best

I love you wife
And I want you here for the rest of our life.

I watched many stories on television and in the movies where two young people got romantic for the first time. The birds were singing, the music playing and everything was just so perfect. One day I said to myself, well that is enough of that, let me write a poem that would account for how things might go if not on television or a movie screen. Remember that humour is a medicine.

The First Time

You have waited for this
Since you shared your first kiss

The candles are lit, the champagne on ice
You primped and you showered
you smell so nice

He walks into the bedroom with a
big smile on his face
Trips over the pants that have
fallen from his waist

He crawls over to you
words of love on his lips
Knees you hard, right in the hips

You let out a painful groan
He mistakes it for a passionate moan

He tries to kiss you reeking of beer
You turn your head he slobbers in your ear

Before you can say stop, wait
He is doing his best to mate

Sadly you realize, long before he speaks
The spirit is willing but the flesh is weak

You try to comfort him, tell him its all right
Then you realize
he has passed out for the night

The saddest part isn't
that this was the first
The saddest part is
he's not even the worst.

Unconditional

You were there when I came screaming
into the light
You said it was love at first sight

You loved me when I first began to walk
You showed such pride on the day I started to talk

Together we shared many days of fun
In your eyes, I was number one

I remember joking and laughing with you
I remember the private talks
that were just between us two

You told me you loved me and left no
reason to doubt
You taught me what true happiness was all about

When other kids hurt me or treated me cruel
You would sit in your car and
wait for me after school

When life took me by surprise
You were there to dry my eyes

You said your love was forever, no matter what
I guess forever isn't as long as I thought

I know I'm not the person you thought I would be
Every time I look in your face
it's disappointment I see

I am genuinely sorry I don't make you proud
And it's all I can do not to scream out loud

I know you don't want me near
You have made it painfully clear

But before I turn to go
There is something you should know

You made a promise to me
That your love was mine, unconditionally

I am not always proud of the things you do
But I will never stop loving you.

Good Night

When I was small enough to cradle in your arms
you kissed me good night
I could feel the love

When I got older you kissed me good night and
said I love you
I said it back and meant it just as much as you

As I aged you said I love you and
kissed me good night
I gave you a passing kiss and mumbled
I love you too

I entered a new school and still you
kissed me good night

I tolerated the smooches because you are my mom
When I became a teenager, it was
not cool to kiss you

So I nodded and said good night, though you did try

When I moved away, you called for the first week
straight to say good night
I did miss you, so once again it was okay to say
I love you and good night

When I found the man of my dreams and married.
you called one more time for that good night
And I was happy to hear from you and happy to
hang up and go to my husband

Then it was my turn to kiss my children good night
Only then did I realize, wow this is what
my mom did, this is how she felt

Good night does not mean good night
it means so much more
It is not just a kiss and words
it is a promise of forever

It says I love you, I am proud of you, you are my
world, my hopes, and my dreams
It means I will always be here
up or down, good or bad
I will always love you unconditionally

Now that my mom is gone
the one wish I will always wish
Is to be able to kiss her and say good night
one more time

Never stop kissing your kids good night.

To My Friend
Gary Norman LaForme

I accept my passing
I am aware of the loss, of the grief I have caused

I shall miss each and every one of you
My wife who I teased, but who made each day that
much better just by being

My children, how I love you and how proud I am
My grandchildren the apples of my eye,
and my favourite past time

My family, my friends
Many of whom are each and the same

Do not leave me flowers, words or tears
Leave me with the knowledge that those
I love will be cared for

For that is all I have ever wanted
To see you happy, healthy, and loved

I hold no anger for that is not my way
The door before me holds no fear
nor does it offer only loneliness

Death cannot take me from you nor you from me
For I am immersed in every part of you

Whenever you look in a mirror or into
each others eyes I will be there
Reminding you of the greatest gift
I have given to you.

Aakwaadewin/Courage

"Found in the dark, in the light, in the shadows, in the sun, in the child, in the adult, in the heart and soul, in nature, and in our ancestors."

I jokingly state that the Government of Canada is crazy putting these seven challenges in front of the Indigenous people, because no matter the obstacle we adapt and overcome, they are creating a world of super-Indigenous people.

I celebrate our ancestors, the men and women, the children who gave so much so that we could stand here today. It takes courage to walk in the tall grass.

Walk With Me

We ask that you would accept us
For we stand ready to accept part of your grief

To share your loss as if it was our own
In writing these words my people have made you
family, in our hearts, in our souls

We pray that by sharing your grief we can
lessen your burden ever so slightly
And help you find a reason, a way to cope
to continue on

We ask the creator to shelter you
To keep you, to give of himself

We ask that we may share your loss
And give you a piece of our life

So that in this moment of greatest mourning
You are never far from our thoughts, never alone

For you and yours reside now
within the heart of my people

Forever.

Hero

A hero is often described as someone
who risks his life for another
And yes this is heroic and we rightly bestow our
gratitude and respect

Yet you are surrounded by heroes every day
People who receive very little acclamation for their
passion and commitment

Those who will not sit back and watch
Those who go above and beyond duty
and obligation
Those who believe in what they do
And through this faith, make others believe

Where success is not measured in
mass or even in money
It's measured by a twinkle in the eye or
a smile on a face

Where it is not about numbers
But the accomplishment of others

A hero cannot always be identified by the
lives they save
Sometimes it is by the lives they touch.

I Love This Land

You were and always shall be my brother
We were all the same colour wrapped in
the flag of this nation
My blood flowed as freely as yours, mixed in the fields
one could not be distinguished from the other

Yet when we came home, when the
nation's colours were removed
Differences became apparent, not between
you and me, god willing never
But in the eyes of those for whom we
laid down our lives

Oh, we still stood shoulder to shoulder in the parades
but the government thought that your life was
more valuable than mine
So you were given land and property, while I waited
and waited, I know what you were given
was not enough for what we endured
Still it was much more than I

I am not envious of you brother, I believe you deserve
even more than you received
But it hurt me very badly, I am not ashamed to say
I cried and why not
I bled, I died, I killed, why does my country
think I am unworthy

The enemy I fought could never be as cruel as the
people I came back to embrace
I gave so much, lived through so much and then you
you who I would give all for, you pushed me aside
as if I was inconsequential
I feel as if I have been spit upon by one I honoured

Do I feel good having to ask you for what should
have been given long ago? no
In fact I am a little ashamed to ask for justice in this
For I never went to war for money, for glory, for
reward, I went because it was the right thing to do and
God forgive me, I would go again

This may seem an old wound to you
but it is a wound that never heals
For it is a wound to my people's heart and soul
an insult to our pride
And we deserve so much better
especially from you.

*I was at a Chiefs of Ontario meeting in 1998 and a Chief and a
Nurse stood up and asked the assembly to support the investigation
into the killing of an unarmed Indigenous man who was standing
in defence of his land. They spoke only briefly, but I was inspired by
their words and I flipped over my agenda and wrote a poem called
"To Fall in Honour is to Rise in Glory." While everyone else went
for lunch, I wrote and when I had almost completed the poem I
started to wonder around and found myself at the back of the room.
People started to return and to avoid the rush I sat in the back row
of the room. As fate would dictate, just as I finished the poem the
Chief and the Nurse who had so inspired me sat on either side of
me and I was able to share the poem they inspired at the moment
I completed it. What is astounding is that they should have been
sitting in the front row and I should have been in the middle rows.*

To Fall in Honour is to Rise in Glory

Sometimes a man must take a stand
I raised my voice in defence of our land

I took up no arms, I attacked no one
I simply raised my voice to the creator, and
lifted my head with pride to the sun

I told you no, you'll take no more
I spoke loudly, yet never did I threaten war

I sang the songs passed down to me
With pride in the open, for the world to see

With righteous honour, I stood in pride
Honouring a tradition, that I would not hide

A shot rang out and I lay dead
A man shot me in self defence
defending himself from words I said

My family and people suffer for
they cannot understand
When they see the taking of a life
punished with a slap on the hand

Was the punishment so minor because
of the colour of my skin?
Is the government hiding, unwilling to admit
they committed this sin?

In their narrow vision they will never see
Their apparent victory, was really a victory for me

I wish to tell my people not to grieve
For in killing me, they have made it impossible
to force me to leave

Would I do it all again, knowing how it would end
As quickly as a leaf is picked up by the wind

Others would ask why
Knowing you will die

Yet I know my people would take my hand
For sometimes a man must take a stand.

Fallen Hero

So many gave so much
To preserve our way of life

So we build our shrines and we lavish praise
We dedicate days and occasions to
our fallen heroes

We put them in the ground, place a
monument over them
And once a year we dig up their memory

We brave the wind, we huddle in the cold
we pay our respects
And hope the service doesn't last too long

Such is the reward of a fallen hero.

The next poem is about a little girl and her family. She developed a very aggressive cancer and she and her family found that the cure was killing her. The family made a choice to stop the treatment and seek alternative medicine, Indigenous medicine. The doctor who was treating the young girl was horrendous and treated the other siblings and the young girl's parents terribly, threatening the very loving family with CAS and Court — right in front of the other young children and the young girl with cancer. Over time, the response changed and the government and the hospital came to support the concept of Indigenous medicine. The doctor who treated the young girl did not change his opinion but modern medicine looked at Indigenous medicine and acknowledged and supported the value. Yet for me, that is not enough. We must never forget this little girl who changed the way conventional medicine thinks of Indigenous medicine. I want her memory to live on, I want people to understand who she is. Mckayla's name deserves to be in the history books. She wanted to be a doctor, and when I asked the hospital if they would do a scholarship in her name they said no. I am determined to see that her name is not lost to time.

Mckayla

Courage is not exclusive to those who fight in wars
or those who protect our streets
Courage is not exclusive to those who run into
burning buildings, or those first on scene

Courage is not about strength of arms
nor is it about reasoning or logic
Courage is not limited to adults

Courage can be found anywhere, anytime
it can come in all shapes and sizes
Courage is not always rewarded, sometimes
it is just the opposite

Courage is not always easily seen sometimes it
shies away from wondering eyes
Courage is not measured by success or reward
sometimes it is quiet conviction

Those who know no fear are fearless, people who
know fear and overcome are heroic
Fearlessness is to be admired, but
heroic is inspirational

And I have seen heroic, I have seen inspirational
And it came in the form of a child

A beautiful yet timid smile
A little girl who knew fear and who made a choice

So strong in her faith, her hope, her belief
Wise beyond her years and gone far too soon

A community and a Nation that said
we love and support you
And your courage, your conviction, inspire us

And that inspiration provides us
strength and unifies us
For a moment in time you have made a family
out of our community, united us as a people

Maybe that unity is fleeting
maybe the moment will pass
But your memory shall remain

The appearance of a young child
But the heart of our bravest warrior

I offer you my love and I wish you peace
And I pray that we can make you as proud
as you have made us.

Victory

Not all victories are won on the playing field
A man who can hold his head high
Accept defeat with honour and dignity
Can be in no way classed a loser

A man who knows he has given his all
Should feel no shame in loss
For another day dawns, another game begins
Losing is merely life's way of teaching

It is exhilarating to face a
worthy opponent and triumph
Yet victory should always be tinged
with the tiniest part of regret
For the way a man wins is more
important than if he wins
True victory goes to the man who knows
how to win and how to lose.

Remember

To all those who came before
To all the people that went to war

To the men and women who faced death
To those who will never again draw breath

To the mothers and fathers whose children gave all
To the husbands and wives whose mate
answered the call

To the children who faced life on their own
To everyone who talks to a name on a stone

No medal and ribbon can repay all that we owe
The parade and applause are not enough
and we know

How do you thank someone for everything you have
and everything you are
Without you, never could we have accomplished so
much or come so far

I don't know how to say thank you
No words are enough for what you went through

There is one promise that I can give
One oath that I will never break as long as I live

I will remember that we owe all to you
A person. A people that I never even knew

I will remember.

Miigwech/Thank You

Whether they fight on the ground, in the air,
or on the water
They are soldiers, they are warriors

They are brothers and sisters, husbands and wives
mothers and fathers, sons and daughters they are the
people of this land and they call Canada home

They leave their lives and their loves
in defence of this land
They share similar traits, heart, courage, love
and dedication to duty

Yet, they are all individuals with their own lives
their own beliefs
Their colours may differ, their insignias may differ

Yet they are all one
Wrapped in the flag of this nation

They are brothers and sisters
who may argue with each other
Yet they will brook no insult to family or country

Some return but not all, and you and I
May never see their face or hear of their deeds
or see where they fall

We may never understand the life they live,
or the life they give
Yet we owe all to these men, these women
their families

And we say thank you, thank you may
seem like small words
But they are all we have and they come
from the heart

Thank you, Miigwech.

Dbaadendizwin/Humility

HUMBLE IS SEEING and understanding the world around you and your place within it. Humble is sharing what you have. To walk in humility is to understand who you are. To understand your spirit, your heart.

Do not judge in haste, do not label at a glance. For the saddest tale that I have ever been told hid behind dancing eyes and a beautiful smile.

To walk in humility is not to be small it is the knowledge that everything is equal.

Clowns

I saw a man with a smile
So I thought him happy

I saw a lady with a frown
So I thought her sad

I saw a lady dance in joy
What a carefree and crazy soul

I saw an accountant at his desk
What a boring life

I saw a man drive a fancy car
So I thought him rich

I saw a lady beg in the street
So I thought her desolate

If we judge another on the basis of appearance
We judge on only what we are allowed to see

For the surface is merely a shadow of the soul
A shadow that rarely reflects the truth

Even someone we think we know so well
Could be the opposite of what we perceive

For sometimes the performance is so wonderful
That the performers can even convince themselves

If we see a clown do we think that he is just a clown
Momentarily we laugh, but we know
he has another life

What does the clown hide behind the
mask of laughter
Is he truly gay and happy?

Does an evil soul hide behind the mask
Does a gentle person wear the paint

Do not judge in haste
Do not label at a glance

For the saddest tale I have ever been told
Hid behind dancing eyes and a beautiful smile.

River of Tears

Children came to me and I embraced them
As is my way, for I have no choice

They did not come willingly
And I did not want to embrace them
yet that it is all I know

And so I took them
Not wanting to, not wishing to

I cannot give them back
I wish so much that I could, but I cannot

I will cry every day, for them
I will weep forever

Every time I embrace a child
My heart breaks upon the shore

The river flows with my tears
I cannot stop this, you must, please

This is not who I am meant to be
Not what I was made to do

Innocence should play along
my shore, and smile in the sun
Not die in my depths alone and afraid.

My Path

I am not a man who lived my life
by society's convention
I travelled my own path in life

Sometimes the roads I travelled were dark
lonely and frightening
I have seen and done things that
I would not wish on another

Yet as the darkness surrounded me
I walked toward the light

I made peace with my past
And lived my life, the best I knew how

Maybe not everyone whose life I touched
has forgiven me
But I have managed to forgive myself

And I found contentment at the end
I wish to say thank you to those who stood
beside and behind me

To those who haven't forgiven me
I offer my sincerest apologies

I wish you all full lives
And I want you to know

I walk toward the light still.

She Was There

I made it to be with you,
I tried it to stay with you
It was a choice filled with risk

But even one day more made it worth the effort
I awoke to the pain, I lived with the indignity

I survived but inside I cried
was it worth it, was it?
I will never do it again
I love life but this again
I will not do

Yet I live, and there you are
So many days, and not one without a smile

I did what I wanted to do
I lived how I wanted to

Yet the pain came again
And the choice came again

And I said I won't do it
But I had to do it, for you were there

So once more I took the risk
Once more I did what I swore not to do

And this time I did not survive
This time the extra time was not to be

This time I did not wake
I tried, but I could not

And when the time came to say goodbye
you were there
And when you told me to let go, I did
for you, as much as me

And as the world tumbled away, and as you
disappeared from my mind's eye
I felt loss, I felt despair for no longer
would I be here or you be there

Yet as I passed from this life and my eyes
closed to this world forever
And the loved ones I left behind mourned me

I opened my heart to the world beyond
And she was there.

Look Again

You see a beggar in the street
You cross over so your paths don't meet

You try to avoid these dirty bums
Begging in the street for another man's crumbs

They accost you day after day
You do your best to simply walk away

You look at them with contempt and disgust
You throw them a dollar when your
conscience says you must

Yes I know what's going through your head
This poor bastard would be better off dead

When you look at me
I know exactly what you see

Because I remember what I used to see
When I was you and I looked at me.

Infinity

Death is given power in prose, in poetry
in history, in life
Death is lamented every day and every night

Whether you're happy and healthy
sad and desperate
Death claims you when death is ready

So much power is ascribed to death so much finality
Even those close to god preach, death
waits for no man

Yet sometimes so much power in life is
given to cause
That the cause goes beyond death
ability to interfere

When a person's hopes and aspirations are carried
on even after he is gone
When a memory is kept so live by those left behind

Death does not become the end of a dream
And when the dream lives on, the memory
and the man live on

A life may be finite and death may be forever
But sometimes even death must wait on a man.

If Corners Could Cry

If corners could cry
The weeping would fill oceans

Silent witness to stolen chances
The squeal of breaks, the twisting of metal
the silence that is death

A mother grieves over the loss of her child
And suffers the agony that only
a mother can know

A father regrets every word spoken in anger
Rage, anger, guilt, weakness, helplessness

A family weeps for the sudden emptiness
Stunned and angry that he is gone

Friends cry over the missed company
Loneliness overtakes them, even in a crowd

So many dreams and ambitions
that will now go unfulfilled
So many things left undone, so many
things left unsaid

Remorse and guilt abound
Harsh words are given far too much credence

Some would argue that god takes what the
world does not deserve
Small comfort

When a room sits empty, when a meal
goes untouched
When a life goes unlived

Every inch of flesh torn by steel, every drop
of blood shed by asphalt
Silent witness to stolen chances

If corners could cry
The weeping would fill oceans.

If I Didn't Have You

If I didn't have you, where would I be
if I didn't have you, who would I be
The way I dress, the way I walk, the things
I think, the way I talk
I am a reflection of the person who shaped my life

Whenever I shed a tear, you dried my eyes
Every sob that wracked my body, you hugged away
All the world's demons, didn't exist in your light

Your arms, your hands held me and
brought me comfort
Your voice and your laugh are the memories
I cherish
And your smile still brings me joy

You thought I couldn't see, when you cried for me
You thought I would think you weak, but all I could
see was a heart that could speak
And someone who would lesson my pain,
no matter the cost

If you didn't show me, how would I know, if you
didn't protect me, how would I grow
I am me because of you, I am strong because of you
and I will succeed because of us
My future is bright and I want to say thank you for
making that possible
You are the one I look up to, the one I see
in all my memories
You are the foundation, on which I built the world
that surrounds me
Although you didn't have to be
you were everything to me.

Let My People Rest

My heart saddens, my eyes mist, my soul screams
My people cannot be left in peace, even in death

Are you so far away from your soul, so far removed
so far out of touch
You cannot see the inherent evil you do

Is money and advancement more important
then loved ones
My leaders, my children, grandchildren, parents

Should I get a shovel and desecrate
those you honour
Must I make you suffer the same indignities to
open your eyes, must I

But I cannot
I have too much respect for all people,
for your people

So much pain has been inflicted upon us
on our ancestors
That we would never willingly inflict it upon
another, but you must stop

By digging up their bones, disturbing their peace
You do the equal of spitting in a child's face of
striking our mothers

You do my people more dishonour in this
a single moment, a single act
Than all the horrors that have been perpetrated
upon my people

I ask you to take one second, stop and
look at what you do
If you cannot see this as a horror

Then you are no longer a man but an empty vessel
You may walk around but you have no soul
you are merely a shell

And you will never realize what you do
And I pity my people, but I pity yours more.

Time is the Enemy

My journey nears its end
The completion of my life begins

Looking back on my past
I sense my future fading fast

I see the times I laughed and cried
I see the times I loved and sighed

I see some places ruled by anger and fear
I see the time when death was near

I see the wrong roads that I've taken
Seen all the good so easily forsaken

So many tasks left incomplete
So many goals I didn't meet

A wife who deserves better than I gave
Greed and jealousy made me their slave

A man who wouldn't listen to what you had to say
Is it any wonder I couldn't get you to stay

Children who really needed their dad
Raised by a father who didn't mean to be bad

I always meant to take you there and teach you this
To be best friends is what I wished

Somehow I thought we would have forever
I wanted you to have the love I never

Somehow I let life's little things get in the way
I'm sorry, just doesn't seem to be enough to say

Lonely and bitter is how I must end
But don't pity me my friend

I chose all those paths,
I let all the opportunities go by
I lived my life with my eyes opened wide

So I bid the world a final goodbye
I make my peace before I die

To my wife, I miss you more than words can say
To my children, you will be a
better man than me I pray

I envisioned a life of love and bliss
But time is the enemy of man's happiness.

Nbwaakaawin/Wisdom

THE DICTIONARY DEFINITION of Wisdom or sapience is the ability to think and act using knowledge, experience, understanding, common sense, and insight. Yet wisdom is the ability to understand that there is knowledge in life and wisdom in everything.

We are all of creation, we are all brothers and sisters, yet we see each other as separate as apart. We are all connected, to the universe, to the world, to each other. We continue to see ourselves divided by policy and geography forgetting the fact that what happens to one eventually happens to all.

My people are divided further, we no longer see ourselves as a nation of Anishinaabe, and we see ourselves as communities, as groups, as organizations, as independent. We see ourselves as the North and the South, as East and West.

My people have lost our way, our perspective. How are we to help one another when we forget we are of one people? When my people heal, it will be because we understand our relations to each other. We need to realign and reconnect as nations as people before we can come together for the benefit of all.

This may seem a conflict in statements but it is not. We have, as the human race, moved so far apart from each other that we need to take the proper steps to come together. Understanding who we are, individually, as nations, as countries, as continents, as the world, are all part of the next step.

Never forget that we are all in this together.

Why Me

Life is a journey
Each stage of life a step in that journey
Yet each step is also its own destination
So that every moment should be special

People must always find their own path
We may try to guide, assist, but no more
For a man to be a man, he must take his own steps
He must follow his own path

And sometimes that path is tough
For life doesn't care about being fair
Doesn't always follow rhyme or reason
Life is just life

Many find this journey a terrible struggle
And endless chaos of confusion
Yet some are blessed to realize
It's a path as any other path

It is not good, it is not bad, it is just what it is
A road to be run or a path to walk
Yet we decide which
In that moment our destiny is our destiny

I am not saying we control the future
Or that we control time
But we can choose the moments of our journey
To feel the wind in our face, the sun in our eyes

And if the journey ends abruptly
If we are taken unawares
We know we have run and walked that road
Because we owned it

So remember me
Not with head down and eyes closed
But with a smile on my lips, a wave to the crowd
Picture me as I made my way down my path

Remember me with my eyes wide open
My path in this world may be done
But the journey will continue
And this time I might choose to go shoeless.

No Greater Gift Than a Friend

People pass in and out of our lives on a daily basis
Friendships are many, but they are fleeting

A hand extended in friendship is always
available when you are up
But when you are down that same hand is
hard to find

Yet there is no blame to give
There is no judgment to be passed
it simply is the way of things

So if you cannot make the time when I need you
If you can only fit me in according to your schedule

I understand, it is the way of things
And the world will still judge us friends

For life is filled with personal and
professional battles
We all must meet at different times in our lives

It is understood that you are my friend
and I am yours

That when we can, when the world allows
we will be there for each other

Yet there are those who come into our lives
And stay through the good, the bad, and the ugly

Who do not wait on the world to make the time
Who will put your needs above their own

So in a world where acquaintances are
now classed as friends
What do you call a true friend, a real friend?

I am lucky for my friend already comes with a name
And I call ....

Dedicated to my sister,
the strongest woman I have ever met
and the most stubborn.

A Special Soul

You have never been one to complain
You smile and the smile hides your pain

Others are used to you being so strong
How could they know, this time they are wrong

I know you will struggle with all your might
I know you will never give up the fight

And god willing you will prevail
Yet if you should falter, if you should fail

If death's dark hand should steal you from sight
I know that a soul like yours
exists forever in the light.

Sometimes Enough is Enough

The weakness of man is his inability
to appreciate what he has
If man has everything he wants more
Yet take everything away and he wishes
he but had it back

We find it so much simpler to cry over
a glass of spilled milk
Than to appreciate the full glass before it topples
It seems the only way man may appreciate
something is in its absence

We never realize how much we really care,
until it is taken away
Our family, our children, our life
all go unappreciated
It seems the phrase 'live for the joy of the moment'
has been replaced by the agony of regret

We get some kind of perverse joy out of our
own sense of loss
Why it is more socially acceptable to
weep over a lost loved one
Than to express your love and appreciation while
that person still lives

It is great to aspire and reach for the stars
But not at the cost of what we have
For believe it or not, sometimes enough is enough.

The Fairy Tale

The romantic beginning, the happy ending
The dreams of every woman, and every man

Since the time our mother or father
read us the first fairy tale
When we watched our first cartoon,
Disney's wonderful world of make believe

Every movie where the hero gets the girl
Every made-up magical moment

Has conditioned us into believing that we
deserve the fairy tale
The white knight on his steed, the beautiful
damsel in the iron castle

The world has force-fed us the idea, the
perfect picture of life
And unlike Santa Claus or the tooth fairy
this childhood tale does not fade

People search all their lives
Passing by happiness in search of a quest,
a dream, our dream

Happiness isn't hard to find but it's hard to hold
Reality is a brutal affront to a fairy tale

Tell me you're a realist, you understand the world
That fantasies and fairy tales are for children

But deep down, where the secrets
we hide in shadow exist
Lies this dream. This idea. This perfect world.

Leader

I respect the wisdom of our elders
I believe in the future that is our children

I am swayed by wisdom
Not words

I cannot be bullied
I may flinch, but I will not cower

Wrong is wrong, whether it is the bare truth
Or whether it comes
disguised in a suit of money

The decisions I make are my own
Not another's

I may be one man
But I am my man

I was elected by my people
To serve my people

And never shall I forget
Every decision I make, must be a reflection of
your need, your desire

Our belief systems
Are my guiding principles

See me speak, hear my words
If I do not do you justice, speak to me, let me know

I do not fear you
Nor should you fear me

I am your voice
I am your servant

I do not believe that I know best
But I believe I know the heart of my people.

Our Nation

I am tom between responsibility and morality
It is my honour and obligation to
better my community

If the betterment of my community must come at
the expense of another then so be it
It matters not if others need it more, I must fight
for all I can get

My ultimate goal is to see streets paved in gold and
money fall from too-full pockets
Even if my brother is forced to live on the streets
and exist on pocket change

This is what I have learned from the others who
lead our nation
That it is the responsibility of good government
to better your own

We scream at the government, honour us,
always we say us
Yet as soon as there is a small amount of
money to be claimed us becomes me

I am tired of scrambling to beat my brother
out of his chance
I don't want to march into the future if my brother
stays in the past

I wish to say brother if truly you need it
more than me, it is yours
Yet I would be considered a fool and a poor leader of
my community

If I were to say, brother I will step back while you
have a chance
My own community would turn on me
in anger and rage

Greed was never the way of our people
Yet it seems we adapt well to the ways of
those who surround us

I know we all need more in our community
and we always will

Yet there are those among us whose need is
greater and far more desperate

Others would call me a fool for wanting to
help your people before my own

Yet I truly believe, there should be no
yours and mine, just ours.

I want to respectfully acknowledge Canada's sesquicentennial and remind Canada that my people have called this land home for thousands of years and not to forget our voices during your 150.

As I am sure you are aware, many Indigenous people feel they should not celebrate the sesquicentennial and this is my attempt to give a voice to those people. Canada must understand that there is anger and the Indigenous people have a right to that anger.

Sesquicentennial

We will celebrate a land, a place that was a dream to my people and became a place that others dreamed to come too

We will celebrate a way of life that respected nature
We will celebrate and embrace those who love and cherish the land

We will celebrate our past for the past is our greatest teacher
We will celebrate our children for they have our love

We will celebrate a relationship that could,
but does not yet exist
We will celebrate your children for they too
have our love

We will celebrate the future for we have faith
We will celebrate a country where we
stand hand in hand

We will celebrate a belief in freedom
We will celebrate those who will
not stand idle

We will celebrate democracy and equality
We will celebrate all those who gave so much
that we could stand here

We will not celebrate the sesquicentennial
We will not raise a glass, light a candle
or whistle a tune

We will not celebrate until Canada becomes
what it once was
We will not celebrate until Canada becomes
what it could be

continued ...

... continued

When we, all of us are equal
When we have taught our children to
value each other

When greed and corruption are finished
When water and land are valued above
the mighty dollar

When the rights and liberties of all people
are protected

When all the people of this land stand
and say enough

We know who we are, and we know
our worth

We know the value of the ground
on which we stand

On that day we will all celebrate.

I think we cannot go forward without looking back, if we are to celebrate let us do it with the knowledge that we celebrate the tenacity of our people, we celebrate a movement to reconciliation, and we utilize Canada's 150 celebration to help bridge gaps and raise awareness, so that we can move toward reconciliation.

One of the things Canada took away from my people was a right to choose how we dressed, what language we spoke, our appearance, even who our people were. I would never take away the opportunity for our people to choose and those who choose to celebrate or participate in Canada's 150 must be respected. I will be part of the 150 because I cannot afford to let this opportunity pass.

Untitled

What do you see when you look at me

The world will judge and we will all be
found wanting
Because the greatest trait we all share is
that of imperfection

So judge my size, my shape, my intellect, my clothes
the way I walk, the way I talk
The colour of my skin, or my religious choice

Laugh if you must, point if you will
For a moment, I may be hurt, for I am human

However, I know my truth and your judgement
on me is only your judgement on me
There was a time, when words could cause me pain

When my face was washed in tears
When I thought the world could see
all my internal scars

Living my life in the shadow of another's scorn
But that stage is done

I feel for the young who do not yet realize the truth
Who can be hurt by the judgement of others

I would comfort them and I do try
Sadly, the truths they are to find will come in their
time, if they come

For sometimes so harsh are the words of others
And so much value is given to such useless words

That the victim cannot continue
And seeks their release through death

And we should mourn for everyone lost
Makes us less than we are

Still I pity the one who casts the abuse, I should not
for it devalues their existence
Yet I find I cannot help it

For though some are lost to the words of others
And cannot find their truth and
the world claims them

Many do find the strength and help others
to find their truth
Even the abuser can find the truth
but it is always tinged

For they must live with the hurt and
destruction they have sowed
Never to forget that such small-minded words cost
all of us so much

I can tell you the truth but it will
not matter until you find it
Still, I would share it with you at every opportunity

What do you see when you look at me
At the end of the day it only matters what I see
when I look at me, and I see from the inside.

Mnaadendimowin/Respect

IF YOU NOTICE the picture at the beginning of this book, and the vignette on the opposite page, you will see I am wearing a ribbon shirt. I wear that shirt, or ones similar to it, on a daily basis.

A man came up to me in the store and said, "That is a nice shirt" to which I replied "Thank you." He continued, "Um, it takes a certain kind of man to wear a shirt like that." I chuckled and again said "Thank you." The truth is when I was young I would have been too afraid to dress like that, too afraid of what people would think or say but the fact is we should not have to change to fit into society, the world around us should adapt to embrace our uniqueness.

We must not only respect diversity we must welcome it, for diversity is how we grow, how we become better today than we were yesterday.

Smile

May you attain everything in life
that your heart desires
May your hurt be small and your joy in abundance

May you find true love that never leaves your side
May you live a long life filled with contentment

May your regrets be few
And your dreams many

May you look back upon your past in
age and be of good cheer
May your family and friends celebrate your life

May you find love and peace
And if I can leave you with one thing

Besides my best wishes and my love
Pursue no dream where there is no smile.

Idle No More

I am an ideal, I am a vision

I am the heart and soul of a people

I embody the past, yet I embrace the future

I am not confined by boundaries of nature or man

I am a million voices and growing

I am the voice of nations

I am the scream of the young

I am the cry of the old

I am an expression of will

I come from the past

I live in the present

I am hope for the future

I am the rhythm of this country

I am idle no more.

The Right Road

I have walked this path for many years
Strayed down the wrong road, a time or two

Yet always did I find my way back
to the Right Road
As a child, I had my parents to steer me

As a teenager I made sense of those wrong turns
But my parents were a guidepost to the Right Road

Then I met you, a beautiful smile and dancing eyes
And my path was no longer my path, but ours

And we walked and we ran and we
danced down our path
And then more came to join us on the path
that we travel

And it was our joy to guide them
in their own direction
And we have so much love and pride
in the path they have taken

The Right Road not an easy road
but a road that leads to fulfillment
A journey worth every step, every struggle

Now we enjoy the sight of our children
guiding their children
And we can smile, relax and continue on

Hand in hand, arm in arm, smile for smile
I wonder sometimes where the
end of the road leads

Is there a garden, is there a dream made flesh
And I realize it doesn't matter
for I know the end of our path
lies in each other's arms

And I thought life was a a journey
down along road
But I have come to understand that
my path was you

Not a journey, an adventure, a life, family,
a love, a connection
I realize that I need not have moved, for my journey
my Right Road, was complete on the day
you said yes.

Belief

We have lost so much and so many
And it seems we lose more everyday

So needed and gone far too soon
I want them all back, even if only for a moment

Loss, grief and hurt threaten to overwhelm
Yet it would not do you justice, to lose hope
and we will do you proud

We may do it with a broken heart and tears
streaming down our face
But we will stand with our head held high
We will be not ashamed to cry

We will earn your respect, we will be worthy
of your memory

We will remember you, honour you
And all that we become, you shall be a part of

For you are a part of our past, our present
And you will be a part of our future

When our children sing their songs
speak their language
When we stand united, when we become
who we are meant to be

We know you will see, we know you will
share our joy
We know you will feel it and we know
you will smile

Your memory shall not be veiled behind the years
It will shine as the stars

Your memory shall lead us
As it should, for we are of each other

We are all connected, we are all one
And as long as one stands we all stand.

I Am My Judge

Do not judge me on your scale
For we are not you, and our lives are not yours

You live your life according to your beliefs, your
songs, and your stories, as you must
Yet we have our own way, our own stories, our own
songs, we may lose our path at times

Still we do not belong to you we belong to us
We have allowed you, to make us less
subject us to your way

But no more, time my people stood up
Found our own path, so that we can make
our own future

Your ideology has not broken us, it has
stunned us and hurt us
But it is not complete and it is not lasting

We will sing to our children and pass on the
stories of our ancestors
And when our time on this plain is ended

We will embrace our brothers and sisters
And they will know us as Anishinaabe.

A Prayer

God grant me the time to fulfill my role in life
Give me the courage to face life and
follow in your steps

Grant me the time to teach others as
I have been taught
Grant me the time to set my children on your path

When my tasks are done, when my time upon
this plain is ended
Take me home and shelter me within your heart

Reunite me with those loved ones who have
gone before me
Place me where I may forever watch over my
children and my children's children

Grant my family and friends the knowledge that
death is merely a door
And that one day I shall be there to greet
each and every one of them.

Nationhood

It is not a means to an end it is our
means to the future
It is not about financial growth, it is not about
political clout

These things will come as they must
But nationhood is about who we are
who our children are

It is the recognition that we were and are a
nation unto ourselves
Our nation stems from our shared history, culture,
language and values

First and foremost we are
brothers and sisters, families
No boundaries of land or government tactics
have ever stopped me from being your brother

We have been apart for some time, but no more
It is not right to keep our families, our
communities apart

So we will walk together, we will
rejuvenate our nation
We will take the first step to the past, a past that
will ensure our future

Our first step must be one of education
Education of our shared history
Our elders can provide this knowledge

We must walk before we run, we must
remember and teach
But we must not wait, our people want this,
our children need this

All of our internal issues all our external issues
will be resolved in time
Our fights will be many, but we will win
for we must

Nationhood is not a means to an end
It is the path to our people's future.

A Good Beginning

Where did the time go, seems the years just flew by
Yet I still have you and you still have me

We may both have a few grey hairs
and some wrinkles
It just proves we spent our lives, living

Besides when I look at you I don't see
age or time
I see my love, my partner

I see the one I fancied the day we met
And if you were to look deep enough
you would see it too

You are the one I wed so many years ago
Still my greatest friend, my choice of partner

Did I forget you have flaws
did I change your flaws, no
I just learned that they are part of
what makes you, you

The times we have been apart
have been hardest
For I miss you, oh I may not always
show it to the world, but I do

People may whisper that we have been
together forever
Yet forever is not a thing of man
it is a thing of spirit

Sixty years is merely a good beginning
Our forever is yet to be.

Journey

I am a man, a son, a grandson, a brother,
an uncle, a cousin

A father, a husband, a leader, a follower, a grandfather

I am just a man, with all the failings of our species

Maybe more, maybe less than some

I have dreams and ambitions, aspirations and goals

Mountains to climb, and oceans to swim

Some I will conquer and some will conquer me

Some dreams I will try, and some I will not

And at the end, the world will judge me

Right or wrong, fair or not, it will

Some will raise me up

For in death, much is forgiven and forgotten

In time my memory will fade from the minds
of the world

And the image shall recede even in the minds
of those who love me

Eventually they shall all pass and my grave
will go untended

My life a dim memory only reflected upon as
a point of context for lineage

It is the way of our time and upon the world
in which we live

It is neither good, nor evil, it is only what it is

We, all of us know this, we do not speak of it

Sometimes, we shroud it in the recess of
our minds, but we know

Yet it does not stop us from progress, nor love,
nor reproduction

Even knowing the limitations of our existence

We must ask ourselves why

Why do we do what we do

And the answer makes no difference

It is the seeking of the answer, the question
that has value

Where we end up, will be where we end up

But the journey is ours.

Final Thought (For Now)

I KNOW RACISM, my people know discrimination, we have lived it and we still face it on many levels, but I have always wanted to believe as a world, as a whole, that we are better than that.

Discrimination is not about power or protection, no matter what words you try to use to disguise it. It is about blind, irrational fear and when we allow fear to become more powerful than our humanity we have already been defeated, and there is nothing more to protect. Fear is okay, fear is a part of nature, a part of survival, but it is not and should not be a way of life.

This is about our children, our future; it should always be about our children. About the world, we will raise them in, about the world we will leave them. No child should know fear or hurt because of the colour of their skin or the language they speak, or the things they believe.

And if we ignore this, if we are quiet, then we condone it.

**I LEAVE YOU WITH
THIS FINAL THOUGHT.**

If you do not have a vision
you will never be
more than you are!

About Chief Stacey Laforme

 Stacey Laforme was born on a cold December morning into a life of alcoholism and abuse. At fifteen, he left home and lived on the street, eventually finding a home with both of his grandmothers. He started his first job at twelve years old, eventually going into the family business and joining the iron workers union. He attended college late in life. He retired from iron work and, as he admits, "If I am honest, I was not the best at iron work."

After his mother passed away at the age of fifty, he was elected to council. He ran and was elected Chief of the Mississaugas of the Anishinaabe in December 2015, a few months after his father passed away. Chief Laforme says, "I am dedicated to my people, and to all the people who live within our treaty lands."

In October 2017, Chief Laforme became only the third Honorary Senior Fellow of Massey College, Toronto, joining The Duke of Edinburgh and The Chancellor of Oxford University in the rarest honour the college bestows.

LIVING IN THE TALL GRASS

Poems of Reconciliation